ADVOCATING FOR QUEER AND BIPOC SURVIVORS OF RAPE AT PUBLIC UNIVERSITIES

Kimiya Factory, Coreen Hale, and Taylor Waits

ADVOCATING FOR QUEER AND BIPOC SURVIVORS OF RAPE AT PUBLIC UNIVERSITIES

The #ChangeRapeCulture Movement

The Queer and LGBT+ Studies Collection

Collection Editor

Seuta'afili Dr Patrick Thomsen

First published in 2024 by Lived Places Publishing

All rights reserved. No part of this publication may be reproduced, stored in a retrieval system, or transmitted in any form or by any means, electronic, mechanical, photocopying, recording or otherwise, without prior permission in writing from the publisher.

The authors and editors have made every effort to ensure the accuracy of information contained in this publication, but assume no responsibility for any errors, inaccuracies, inconsistencies or omissions. Likewise, every effort has been made to contact copyright holders. If any copyright material has been reproduced unwittingly and without permission the Publisher will gladly receive information enabling them to rectify any error or omission in subsequent editions.

Copyright © 2024 Lived Places Publishing

British Library Cataloguing in Publication Data
A CIP record for this book is available from the British Library

ISBN: 9781916704138 (pub)
ISBN: 9781916704152 (ePDF)
ISBN: 9781916704145 (ePUB)

The right of Kimiya Factory, Coreen Hale, and Taylor Waits to be identified as the Authors of this work has been asserted by them in accordance with the Copyright, Design and Patents Act 1988.

Cover design by Fiachra McCarthy
Book design by Rachel Trolove of Twin Trail Design
Typeset by Newgen Publishing UK

Lived Places Publishing
Long Island
New York 11789

This book is open access (BY-NC-ND), and the digital files are available to download for free from our website, where you will find information about the license and our open access policy.

www.livedplacespublishing.com

Abstract

Advocating for Queer and BIPOC Survivors of Rape at Public Universities: The #ChangeRapeCulture Movement offers theoretical groundings, model strategies, and practical solutions to understanding how rape culture affects public university culture. In 2019, at the University of Texas at San Antonio (UTSA), #ChangeRapeCulture, created and led by queer Black students, worked to champion the national conversation about rape culture. Since then, the movement has gone from student protests to conferences, workshops, fundraisers, community events, and youth meetings about the reality of rape culture in America.

#ChangeRapeCulture aims to highlight stories from BIPOC, LGBTQIA2S+ survivors; advocate for their rights; and dismantle the harmful stereotypes that disadvantage sexual violence survivors in real life. Every survivor of sexual abuse has a story to tell, and the organizers of #ChangeRapeCulture are willing to risk everything to make sure these stories are being spread to as many people as possible. It happens way more than you think. All you have to do is listen.

Keywords

Education, gender, lived experience, activism, LGBTQIA2S+, sexual violence, student-led movements, culture, stereotype, rhetoric.

Trigger warning

This book contains explicit references to, and descriptions of, situations which may cause distress. This includes references to and descriptions of:

- Suicidal thoughts, intentions, and actions;
- Mention of rape, institutional violence, grooming, and rape culture;
- Psychotic delusions and hallucinations;
- Violent assault;
- Ableism, discrimination, and micro-aggressions; and
- Racial slurs.

Every effort has been made to provide more specific content warnings before relevant chapters, but please be aware that references to potentially distressing topics occur frequently and throughout the book. Please be advised before continuing. If you are looking for resources for queer and/or of-color sexual violence survivors please go to RAINN.org or changerapeculture.org.

Contents

Preface: Sum to say viii

Learning objectives x

Chapter 1 Rape culture at public universities 1

Exercise 1.1: It happens more than you think—script 12

Exercise 1.2: It happens more than you think—large discussion debrief 16

Chapter 2 Living histories: The beginning of #CRC 19

Exercise 2.1: Living history writing exercise 1 —personal histories 28

Chapter 3 Survivor-centered models and a culture of consent 31

Chapter 4 Living histories: Strategy and survival 39

Exercise 4.1: Living history writing exercise 2 —group histories 54

Chapter 5 How to advocate for university student survivors—podcast transcription 57

Discussion topic themes and questions 80

References 82

Recommended further reading 84

Index 85

Preface

Sum to say

Kimiya

It has been nearly five years since changing rape culture changed MY life forever. It initially took me 730 days to accept my story and to be able to tell it—to relive, learn from, and stomach the awful truth that I discovered existed as a junior in college. With only the afro on my head and a bad-ass co-founder, we began Change Rape Culture. As it exists, as it perpetuates itself in society time and time again through acts of structural violence and the oppressive systems that uphold it.

If you have ever been cat-called, this is for you. If you have ever opened up to anyone, just for them to ask you if you're "sure", this is for you. If you have ever heard a rape joke that triggered you so bad you think you might have felt the earth shake, this is for you.

I'll keep going: If you ever had an idea that was "too big", a creepy family member that you always seemed to end up alone with, transphobic parents that refused to accept your identity, a job that silenced your calling out of its patriarchal system—this is for YOU.

DEEP FUCKING BREATH.

I need one. To remember the revelation of a lifetime to share with you all. It's time to fuck some shit up again. For the sake of history, for the sake of those silenced, for the survivors who have to see their rapists on campus, at "family" holiday gatherings, and for the pain we try to wash off in the shower or a hot bath. By telling my story, I hope to provide strength and promise to the eyes that comb over this book. I hope that whoever comes across these words knows that there is someone out there fighting for you. Here goes nothing and something, all at the same time.

Taylor

No matter where you are in your journey with abuse (ally, survivor, still in an abusive relationship), #CRC is there to help. We meet survivors where systems refuse to go: wherever the survivor wants. There is a huge opportunity laid in front of public university students, staff, and faculty members to protect queer survivors of color from all violence(s) including sexual and intimate partner violence. There are opportunities for growth, connection, safety, transparency, and solidarity that empower everyone within the university. While doing this work first among collegiate queer and survivors of color I learned how desperate our work continues to be. We have a slogan: **For Survivors, By Survivors**, because at so many times the only people who are there to help you are other survivors. For the past five years I have had the privilege to watch our work expand past the university and go into homes, community centers, daycares, classrooms, Zoom rooms, bars, and offices across America. Sexual violence and rape culture does not only exist on our campuses—it's in all aspects of our lives. While my first instance of having my voice elevated as a sexual violence survivor was in college, my first assault happened before I was in grade school. We hope you read this carefully. We hope you use this information carefully. And that you leave our book working to protect the unknown survivors all around you.

Learning objectives

1. Define rape culture and describe the obstacles queer and/or BIPOC (Black, indigenous, and people of color) **student** survivors face on and off campus.
2. Recognize the importance of queer and BIPOC storytelling in public university sexual violence and community accountability policy making.
3. Question how rape culture, patriarchy, and gender-based discrimination show up in one's own lived experiences.
4. Experiment with sharing (written, orally, etc.), holding, and investigating one's own experiences as well as other participants' experiences to create new ways of being.
5. Assemble resources for BIPOC and/or queer student survivors.

1
Rape culture at public universities

Rape culture: A society or environment whose prevailing attitudes have the effect of normalizing or trivializing sexual assault or abuse.

Title IX passing

In 1970 only 7 per cent of high-school athletes and 15 per cent of collegiate athletes were girls (Staurowsky et al., 2022). High-school-aged female-identified athletes faced mountains of obstacles compared with their male counterparts, including, but not limited to, raising their own money, funding their own trips, and facing discrimination from institutional representatives and male athletes. These issues were equally complicated for collegiate and professional women athletes. By 1972 women's rights in athletics was made into a federally recognized problem. In 1972 President Richard Nixon signed a federal law known as Title IX after representatives Patsy T. Mink, Edith Green, and Senator Burch Bai introduced it to integrate cisgender women into collegiate and professional sports and uphold women's rights (Winslow).

On the surface Title IX was the answer to integrating federal civil rights discrimination policies into higher education institutions. However, historians like Natalia Mehlman Petrzela insists in her CNN News mini documentary on Title IX that other lawmakers were not as excited for Title IX as they wanted the public to believe. She emphasizes that conservative lawmakers wanted to be able to say that federally funded institutions advocated for equality to continue receiving federal funds (CNN, 2022). However, the funds were not yet designated to be used explicitly to empower collegiate cisgender women athletes and instead were disproportionately used to discourage equal treatment of these athletes. Many lawmakers of the 1970s still held patriarchal sentiments about women in sports and held beliefs that women were physically and mentally unable to be equal to men in general, not to mention male athletes (CNN, 2022). Furthermore, from 1973 to 1977 there were zero women in Senate and between 16 and 19 women total in the House (Rutgers, The State University of New Jersey). This combination of small numbers of governmental representatives and an overrepresentation of representatives valuing patriarchal ideals (heteronormativity, strict gender roles, etc.) resulted in the suppression, devaluation, and finicky treatment of collegiate sexual violence policies, as further explained in Mehlman Petrzela's video (CNN, 2022). The University of Illinois Library details a definition of patriarchy through the lens of queer theory. They define patriarchy as a system of domination that prioritizes a male-dominated society (University of Illinois Library). We at #ChangeRapeCulture believe that lawmakers and university administrators alike simply wanted to support Title IX to pacify the feminist killjoys who insist that a specific distinction be added for how federal funds can be used to protect and empower collegiate survivors.

Pushback

On February 17, 1976, the National Collegiate Athletic Association (NCAA) filed a lawsuit challenging the legality of Title IX (Staurowsky et al., 2022). They claimed that no athletic programs received direct federal funds and thus shouldn't be forced to abide by Title IX regulations. Some even declared they would no longer accept public funds and petitioned privatized collegiate athletics teams. The suit was later dismissed in 1978 (Staurowsky et al., 2022). Later, in 1984 the Supreme Court case Grove City College v. Bell limited the scope of Title IX. Title IX only applied to specific programs that received federal funds (Staurowsky et al., 2022), and under this interpretation, the law did not necessarily cover athletics. This limitation came as a direct pushback to a Title IX policy interpretation done by the Department of Health, Education, and Welfare in 1979 through the Office of Civil Rights. The policy interpretation prohibited educational programs and institutions from being funded if they participated in sex-based discrimination.

The conditions from 1979 were:

1. Athletic financial assistance. Schools were required to award scholarship money to men and women proportional to participation rates.
2. Accommodation of athletic interests and abilities. Schools could satisfy the participation requirement in one of three ways, known as the three-prong test, the first of which was

      by offering athletic participation numbers proportionate to enrollment.
3. Other areas, a laundry list including equipment, practice times, support services, etc.

Despite pushback, the idea that institution "x" received federal funding and would need to allocate funds specifically meant to eliminate sex-based discrimination was reinstated but only in collegiate sports programs. This specific placement for Title IX left every other aspect of collegiate life without allocated support to eliminate gender-based discrimination. Soon, Title IX began to function as a jumping point to discuss gender-based violence on and off campus, inside and outside the locker rooms, and in all departments of the institution.

Title IX over time

These discussions of gender-based discrimination included topics like, but not limited to, sexual violence, transgender rights, and abuse. As rape culture conversations continued to mold and change across public campuses in America, the center of Title IX's focus has gone from integrating women into sports and sexual harassment in the 1970s (CNN, 2022); to adding sexual orientation and gender identities as protected classes in the mid 2010s (U.S. Department of Education, 2023); and dealing with violence between faculty, staff, and students (Know YourIX.org, n.d.). What was the responsibility of the institution to protect those that received harm while attending, working, or interacting with the institution? If a representative of the institution is perpetuating violence, what protocols does the institution take?

During the Trump administration in 2016, Title IX jurisdictions became constricted similarly to the way they were in the 1970s. The administration's additions added up to 2,033 pages (Bedera, 2020). The additions drastically reduced the types of sexual misconduct that universities were required to investigate. And when the investigation started survivors were required to be cross-examined with their perpetrator. If survivors did not wish to pursue an investigation, they could ask for an "informal resolution", which required participation from both parties and no punishments were allowed (Bedera, 2020). Instead of seeking justice, survivors were subjected to more paperwork. This restriction was only temporary, but it influenced waves of federally funded institutions to create extra barriers to reporting sexual violence for women and gender-variant people.

New rules, different problems

In 2021 the Biden administration signed an executive order to propose changes to Title IX and expand protections for trans and queer people. In 2023 with a pandemic, over 340+ bills directly discriminating against mainly trans people but also queer folks in America (Bathroom Bills, Drag Bans, Transgender Athletes, etc.) on the Senate floor, and rising discrimination offenses against LGBTQIA2S+ folks, Title IX restriction conversations have found new focus.

In 2023, the U.S. Department of Education released a fact sheet explaining their proposed changes to Title IX specifically around transgender and intersex student athletes. The Department discourages what they call "one-size-fits-all policies" that remove transgender students in public K-12 and collegiate schools from all sports (U.S. Department of Education, 2023). They instead encourage schools to create well-rounded and specific policies that help students learn about "teamwork, leadership, and physical fitness". Despite the positive goals of including gender-variant students in Title IX protections, public universities are determining the protections centered around the bodies, presentations, and attitudes of transgender students. In 2022, Outsports reporters Cyd Zeigler and Karleigh Webb wrote an article titled "These 36 trans athletes have competed openly in college", to show that cyclical instances of outrage towards trans athletes will not stop them from competing in collegiate sports. They emphasize that trans students have competed and openly withstood public pushback within collegiate sports since 2010 and that "Outsports knows there are countless other trans athletes who have competed at the collegiate level who have not been publicly out or out to teammates". They harp on transitioning being at the center of requirements for many college athletes, as the gender athletes transition to will be how they compete, not the sex they were assigned at birth (Zeigler and Webb, 2022). Ever since 2010 colleges have begun and continue to allow trans men and women to compete on their respective team or have non-gendered teams. Collegiate athletes are coming out as trans more and more each day but mainly because, unless a student comes out, they will not be able to compete on the team of their chosen gender (U.S. Department of Education, 2023). The first out trans man in the NCAA Division 1 was a Black man named Kye Allums who competed on the George Washington University's basketball team (Zeigler & Webb, 2022). He notably came out prior to NCAA's trans athlete announcement in 2011. NCAA Division 2 athletes like track and field athlete CeCé Telfer and fencer Bobbie Fischer competed on athletic teams before, during, and after transitioning genders (Ziegler & Webb, 2022).

Title IX and student eligibility

The question of allowing transgender athletes to participate in sports, from elementary school to professional sports, continues to be a huge topic of conversation globally. In America the specific addition to Title IX that includes transgender students is in Section 106.41(b)(2):

> If a recipient adopts or applies sex-related criteria that would limit or deny a student's eligibility to participate on a male or female team consistent with their gender identity, such criteria must, for each sport, level of competition, and grade or education level: (i) be substantially related to the achievement of an important educational objective, and (ii) minimize harms to students whose opportunity to participate on a male or female team consistent with their gender identity would be limited or denied.

So, if a student identifies as man or woman and meets these criteria they can play? Even though the discretion is still left to school officials to make the final call (KnowYourIX.org). Once again, gender-expansive student athletes who identify as man or woman have certain protections, but how does this work for non-binary and intersex athletes? What about non-athletes' protections?

Despite the 2016 withdrawal of the Department of Education's clarification of queer and trans student survivors' rights by the

Trump administration, queer and transgender students are legally protected by Title IX. This means that transgender students' access to education, dress codes, pronouns, and single-gendered facilities like restrooms are protected (KnowYourIX.org, n.d.). They are also protected from harassment, bullying, discrimination, and sexual violence. However, as society perpetuates rape culture and public institutions mimic society at large, rape, abuse, and domestic violence survivors of color become a consequence, an afterthought, an obstacle to the institution when reporting with Title IX coordinators or mandated reporters (KnowYourIX.org, n.d.).

Obstacles reporting to Title IX

Racialized and queer student survivors face intersectional obstacles when reporting. For starters, 70 per cent of college students (regardless of gender) say they have been sexually coerced (Blackburn Center). Of all those cases, more than two-thirds of them will never report their assault to city or university police (RAINN). According to RAINN, for every 1,000 cases, 975 perpetrators will walk free. The respondents detailed to RAINN researchers fear of retaliation, belief that the police would/could not do anything to help, belief that the assault was a personal matter, reporting to a different official, belief that their assault was not important enough to report, not wanting to get the perpetrator in trouble, and other reasons as barriers to reporting.

Another barrier is that most institutions do not adopt survivor-centered models and instead prioritize the safety of the accused **over** the safety of the student body. For example, according to Title IX policy, if a student is assaulted by another student in an off-campus apartment this report is relegated to the local police department. If the victim does not wish to pursue legal action but does wish to pursue reporting the assault to the Title IX office, few things can be done to protect the survivor. With no proof of an assault having taken place through the police, the university isn't allowed to discipline the alleged assailant (Bedera, 2020). The assailant is allowed to remain on campus to assault again and again while their survivor now has the burden to prove an assault occurred in the first place (Bedera, 2020). Policies that require survivors to present a burden of proof via a police report, rape kit results, or retelling their attacks over and over work to directly dissuade folks from reporting (RAINN). One strategy that our co-founders have personal experience of is cross-examination of survivor stories while their abuser and a team of coaches is present. The purpose of this is to encourage the survivor not to take legal action and instead leave it up to their coaches to administer punishment. This is done for a myriad of reasons, such as keeping funding and funders, keeping key players for athletic prowess, and institutions not wanting to recognize that they employ or promote those accused of harm. Presidential administrations, lobbyists, justice systems, and politicians assist in perpetuating rape culture by relegating the responsibility for justice on to the survivor. Institutions relegate much of the legal burden to not only the survivors themselves, but also local community-run survivor advocacy organizations or school police forces. #ChangeRapeCulture often intervenes to train university officials, police officers, and mental health professionals in survivor-centered models and harm reduction; offer mental health support groups where university mental health resources alienate or further victimize survivors; and collect resources to amplify survivor stories when university officials or lawyers threaten students from speaking out. There was a specific case where a survivor was interviewed by university police with no scheduled follow-up with a licensed mental health professional, which caused them to have a public mental breakdown, resulting in them attempting suicide while on campus in front of others. Bullying from other classmates and threats from their abuser ramped up after this attempt, leading to them dropping out of school. Students report there are no ways to keep them safe other than personal police escort or telling the accused to move around their schedule to avoid seeing one another. Students who are queer, of color, housing insecure, or facing hunger are at higher risk of not reporting and continuing to attend school with their abusers. Institutions protect abusers.

Institutions protect abusers

When institutions refuse to expand their definitions and policies of sex and gender-based violence they send students a specific message: **Don't bother reporting**. Queer and BIPOC students face intersectional obstacles when they report (Kosciw et al., 2022). Queer students do not report due to embarrassment, believing no action would be taken against the perpetuators while simultaneously facing a higher prevalence and underreports of sexual violence incidents. Queer students of color are at higher risk of experiencing violence due to racism and are also less likely to report their assaults (Kosciw et al., 2022). Public universities fail to adopt survivor-centered models for all aspects of collegiate life including Title IX offices. A survivor-centered approach seeks **only** to empower survivors by prioritizing their rights, safety, well-being, needs, and wishes (UN Women, 2011). Organizations that wish to adopt this model must provide appropriate, accessible, and quality services to survivors. However, most universities protect abusers and prioritize the safety of the accused **over** the safety of the student body. Whether it may be to keep funding, to trick community members into a false sense of safety, or just not caring—the negligence is clear. Universities relegate much of the legal brunt to local community-run survivor advocacy organizations or school police forces. They sidestep responsibility for disciplining the accused by claiming not to be able to get involved. Title IX offices offer student survivors a myriad of distancing tactics, none of which result in disciplinary action taken against the accused. The best prevention tactics that universities and university police stations offer are typically things like a personal police escort, or changing the accused's schedule to avoid making contact; and that's after they run their own investigation and determine whether the concern is valid. These methods further the stereotypes that undermine and question survivor stories and perpetuate rape culture. Students who are queer, of color, housing insecure, differently abled, or facing hunger are at higher risk of not reporting and continuing to attend school with their abusers because once again the messaging is clear—**institutions protect abusers**.

One of our survivors detailed an instance where they saw the Chief of Police comforting their abuser. This was days after #CRC co-founders had acted as mediators between the office of the Chief of Police and student advocates on campus where the Chief of Police met with and discussed the specifics of this relationship with the survivor themselves. The Chief made a promise to keep this student safe from their abuser, specifically citing "having Black daughters", only to never follow up with the survivor and meet with the accused several times after the mediation. This abuser then began to stalk their survivor, gaslight them out of speaking out, and called them over 250 times. When this survivor went to follow up with the Chief about the case, they were informed that, because they were a man and the abuser was a woman, "a stern talking to" was all that was needed. With both of these folks being a part of the queer community, the survivor decided to cut everyone at school off and operate in almost complete solitude.

Exercise 1.1: It happens more than you think—script

Objectives: This script should be used as a catalyst in discussions about rape culture on campus, in community, and the world abroad.

Warning: While this script is based on real events, certain discussions may relate to the audience's personal experiences. It is imperative that if a mandated reporter will be present at the conversation, this should be related to all members of the discussion. These conversations should not center alleged perpetrators or be used to intimidate survivors. Like #CRC's experience with hosting a conversation similar to this—it may be best to talk off campus. Prioritize the safety of survivors before discussing the topics brought up in this script. Invite local survivor advocacy groups to offer counselors, advocates, or educators to sit in and help guide this conversation.

Instructions:

1. Establish "Shared Agreements" before assigning roles or reading individually. Establish conversation boundaries, discuss Title IX mandatory transparency, and find ways to respect one another's experiences.
2. Next, offer a myriad of participation methods within the discussion. Due to the triggering subject matter some may choose to participate in silence, virtually, in person, in writing, or not at all. If they ask to leave class please allow them to.
3. Develop a way to read the script. This can be done as a group or individually. Encourage students to process the subject matter in a way that empowers their safety. Inspire them to read in groups, using headphones, walking around, knitting, coloring, etc.
4. After reading the script or during the script prompt questions about the societal prevailing attitudes of normalizing or trivializing sexual assault or abuse.

***

Trigger Warning: Sexual abuse, rape, institutional violence, and grooming.

***

Student 1: Thank you all for reading our Snap messages and our in-person flyers. A few of us have been hearing more and more about repeatedly dealing with their abusers on campus so it was about time we actually talk about it.

Student 2: I won't lie—my abuser is actively trying to get me kicked out so I fully believed this was something he was doing to trick me. So happy I saw you at the door when I walked up.

Student 1: Kicked out? Can I ask you how that is possible?

Student 2: Well, since I was assaulted off campus and didn't go to the police I can be sued for defamation. My abuser's aunt is a lawyer and he keeps sending me threatening messages about telling my parents we f*cked.

Student 3: And HE is trying to get YOU kicked out? Is the school doing anything?

Student 2: Well, I went to the Title IX office but they told me I didn't go to the cops so it's he say she say. The best they can do is ask him to leave me alone. I can't get our class schedules changed without "evidence" of the assault. I don't mess with cops so I just gave up trying to do anything.

Student 4: See, as a gay man I see all these abusers abuse women and then leave the dorms and come f*ck with us on the down low. Most of these people are also hiding their sexuality and that adds into how messed up this all is. My abuser is a soccer player and I heard the girls who tell the coaches first end up getting roasted in this weird coach panel.

Student 5: OH MY GOD THAT HAPPENED TO ME! I got assaulted by a football player and when I told the coach he acted like he believed me and wanted to punish him. He told me to tell him what happened in the coach's meeting room but when I got there the entire coach team was there—plus my abuser. They grilled me about what I wore, who my family is, and whether or not I actually wanted to have sex. They told me they would deal with it. I don't see him as much but he's still on the team.

Student 1: My straight guy friend has been getting verbally and sexually assaulted by this sorority girl we know. He went to the Greek office and was laughed out. Then he spoke to the Police Chief who lied about taking a statement from him. Last week she went to his on-campus job to try and convince him to stop telling officials on campus about her and he ended up having a panic attack in the quad. It sucks because everyone basically tells him to hit her back or man up.

Student 4: See, and if it was two Black men they still wouldn't care. When do they care about rape and abuse victims? If the white girls are getting cease and desist letters the Black and Brown students don't stand a chance!

Student 3: I mean, my Mexican girlfriend was just passed a Scantron by her abuser in class.

Student 2: Wait, what?

Student 3: She didn't think anyone would believe her because she's trans so she just didn't tell anybody. He sits right behind her in every class.

Student 5: Well, what are we going to do? Just keep letting this happen? Keep sweeping it under the rug? Keep allowing the survivors to be burdened with all the shame and hard work?

Student 1: We've been talking to some lawyers we know to see what rights we have. Which, because of America, are pretty few. Unless someone has been convicted of a crime we have to say "alleged" if we share our stories publicly. If we outrightly accuse our abusers we are liable to be sued for libel or defamation. Nothing is stopping us from posting their names next to the word alleged.

Student 2: I want to help but I can't participate with my abuser already on my tail.

Student 4: What do y'all need? I'm there!

Student 3: Ditto! Call me, beep me!

Student 5: I'm tired of feeling like I did something wrong. Let me know the time and place!

Exercise 1.2: It happens more than you think—large discussion debrief

Objectives: This discussion debrief should be used as a pair in discussions about rape culture on campus, in community, and the world abroad.

Warning: While this script is based on real events, certain discussions may relate to the audience's personal experiences.

It is imperative that if a mandated reporter will be present at the conversation, this should be related to all members of the discussion. These conversations should not center alleged perpetrators or be used to intimidate survivors. Like #CRC's experience with hosting a conversation similar to this—it may be best to talk off campus. Prioritize the safety of survivors before discussing the topics brought up in this script. Invite local survivor advocacy groups to offer counselors, advocates, or educators to sit in and help guide this conversation.

Instructions:

1. Use the "Shared Agreements" created for the script and adjust them for a group or online discussion(s).
2. Next, offer a myriad of participation methods within the discussion. Due to the triggering subject matter some may choose to participate in silence, virtually, in person, in writing, or not at all. If they ask to leave class please allow them to.
3. Prompt listed and unlisted questions about the societal prevailing attitudes of normalizing or trivializing sexual assault or abuse.

***

Trigger Warning: Sexual abuse, rape, institutional violence, and grooming.

***

Prompted questions:

1. What are some examples of the university perpetuating, normalizing, or trivializing sexual violence, assault, and abuse?
2. What intersectional obstacles did the queer students express facing?
3. Do you think every resolution the institution enacted follows Title IX regulations? Why or why not?
4. What on-campus resources would you recommend to these students? Off-campus?
5. How do you think the university could better assist these students? How do you think their city or community could better assist students?

2
Living histories
The beginning of #CRC

My jaw clenched and palms sweated as I covered the protests that I was assigned to cover as the assistant news editor for my school newspaper. Brett Kavanaugh had just been appointed to the Supreme Court and the nation was raging with protests after Christine Blasey Ford came forward about being sexually assaulted by the Supreme-Court-Justice-to-be. On my college campus pro-Kavanaugh and anti-Kavanaugh protests were held, arguing the guilt and innocence of this man. Covering these protests as a journalist meant that I had to only take quotes from students and refrain from inputting any opinion for the sake of journalistic bias—writing news during this time was one of the most challenging commitments I had ever made.

On the day that I covered the pro-Kavanaugh protests, I watched frat boys holding signs with rape jokes on them. Cheeks pink from screaming, proudly wearing the letters of their fraternities. I finally stomached the nerve to walk up to one, needing a single quote for the story I was writing.

He proudly spoke into my recording device, "I mean, who cares? It was years ago, she has no proof, and he has earned his nomination. Everyone is overreacting, she's probably lying anyway". My spirit felt like it sank into the ground as I glanced a distance away and spotted one of my classmates wiping giant tears from her cheeks. I walked over to her and whispered in her ear not to cry—that I had a plan.

Two weeks before, I sat across from Taylor Waits on her bedroom floor. We both held cups of Minute Maid juice as we exchanged stories of rape, sexual assault, and abuse that we had heard on campus. At the time, Taylor Waits was the university's annual "Ms", and also a student leader like me. We had access to several testimonies, seeing as we both were very involved in the university's extracurricular community. It was the brutal rape of our mutual friend that lit the fucking flame—Taylor pushed her glasses back onto the middle of her nose as she asked me, "So we're going to do this?"

I didn't know what I was even going to eat for lunch the next day in between classes, but I knew that I was ready to dismantle the patriarchy. Even if it meant that it would cost me and my future everything.

On November 15, 2018, Taylor and I held a meeting titled "It Happens More Than You Think: Let's Talk About It". We relied on word-of-mouth throughout the day in hopes that survivors on campus would come and share the space with us. Our jaws nearly dropped as more people than seats we had available showed up, all with the same fire in their eyes. We opened up the floor and testimony after testimony poured out from each attendee. Soon enough, people at the meeting turned out to have the same rapist in common—presidents of student organizations, star athletes, and professors. I was shaking with rage and we all soon enough were empowered to do SOMETHING, after coming to the revelation that these rapists had patterns and would soon strike again—the least that we could do was offer support to other survivors on campus. Our inaugural letter to the student body reads:

> We, the women of UTSA, are choosing to take a stand against the rampant sexual assault and abuse on campus and around the world.
>
> Rape and abuse culture is strong in America as well as on this campus. Women are often not believed, and made to go through treacherous and traumatic processes, including reliving their abuse for hours in interviews, invasive rape kits, and having their sexual and personal lives being scrutinized by the public.
>
> Men and women give into this disgusting culture by refusing to believe their friends, making excuses for abusers, romanticizing rape and abuse as "things that just happen in relationships", and perpetuating slut culture in order to suppress women's sexuality and re-assert that women's decisions are not their own.
>
> When women come forth and try to report their abusers, they risk physical, mental, or cyber retaliation from their abusers and the community who refuses to believe them. We refuse to give into this culture any longer. We are taking a stand to start 1.) a victim protection against sexual predators and abusers of UTSA; 2.) establish a culture of protection against sexual predators and abusers at UTSA; 3.) issue this public statement to offer women of the same mindset and opportunity to decide whether or not to start combatting this issue.

> As a way to start, we have started an anonymous online reporting system for survivors to vent their experiences with their abuse (hereforyouutsa@gmail.com). To the survivors, we believe you, we love you, and we are so sorry the world has failed you.
>
> We are disgusted that your abusers continue to function on this campus, and that you have to relive your trauma everyday as they get to walk freely amongst society. Women need to start sticking up for one another, believing one another, and most of all, protecting each other.
>
> Let's start today.

At this time, I had stumbled upon the term "praxis" in my years as a cross-examination debater on UTSA's debate team, and little did I know, we are carrying out the very foundation of praxis. Praxis can be defined as "practice as distinguished from theory". For the first time in my life, I had to grapple with the question: What is a movement without praxis? We can't rely on the verb "movement" to do the work. Praxis is necessary for the "flame of the baton" that our ancestors inspire us to carry—I like to say. Upon reflection, Taylor and I realized we had instinctually incorporated the principles of the Combahee River Collective long after we drafted the manifesto and distributed it in restrooms across our college campus. Goosebumps ran up my arm as I read the Combahee River Collective, weeks after we had released our own manifesto.

The Combahee River Collective Statement did exactly what we aimed to do: call out the adherent and subliminal patriarchy and homophobic and sexist tendencies that came with believing survivors. The Combahee River Collective also pointed to the treatment of queer Black people being sidelined or disregarded in the feminist movement as it progressed in history, and a testimony never rang so loud or clear for me. In *Scenes of Subjection: Terror, Slavery and Self-making in Nineteenth Century America* by Saidiya V. Hartman, Hartman discusses the observational writing of John Rankin, who publishes a description on the obscenity of the slave trade, and Hartman calls out the undertones of pervasive, white fragility that the chapters illuminate upon the recognition of the gratuitous violence that Black bodies are forced to endure pre- and post-19th-century enslavement. Hartman writes, "Put differently, the effort to counteract the commonplace callousness to Black suffering requires that the white body be positioned to be in the place of the Black body in order to make the suffering visible and intelligible" (Hartman, 1997). This excerpt of a very telling and true reading really acknowledged the pit at the bottom of my stomach as I would try to carve out an intersectional, safe space with survivors who were not of color that would proudly interject, cut me off mid-sentence of my testimony, and state, "Girl, I know!! I [insert their experience with rape culture]", when it was never the same. And what Hartman and the Combahee River Collective, a group of Black lesbian feminists, were getting at, is that for the Black body to express pain, torture or lack of bodily autonomy is the very instance in which our oppressors—regardless of education, class, or alliance with Black struggle—have to be included to understand. I would even assert an instinctual action rooted in colonization's need and desire to assimilate experiences that are not one's own. This rang so true when queer Black women showed up to our "It happens more than you think, let's talk about it" meeting that created the manifesto because the anonymous reporting stemmed from the rape culture of Black women not being believed. Taylor and I knew how imperative it was even to protect the physical location of the meeting (social media was a bit fresh at this point in our experience of organizing), which was not disclosed until the day-of. We knew from the moment of liberating others that the power in liberation is the fire that could burn our beloved community of survivors scrubbing extra hard in the shower—yearning, burning, and fighting the stench of their rapist's crime. That same fire was evenly matched as a fire that the patriarchy could turn into one of their own agenda. One that could insert danger towards the very people that we are dedicated to—instinctively protecting—Black queer survivors of UTSA. The need to hold a meeting that honored our ancestors' wishes never escaped us. We gave priority to safety, not numbers—and our ancestors gave us BOTH. Survivors who desperately needed a space to be believed in woke us UP. We all woke each other up, our suffering was shared and infinite in the generational trauma and racial rape that our rapists carried.

Photos from the movements
All of these photos were taken between 2018 and 2019.

We then strategized to break up the collective into groups that would physically distribute our statement around various buildings in restrooms on campus—my heart pounded throughout the day as I harbored a roll of tape and flyers in my trench coat.

The private group chat that we created was blowing up with updates from student workers that the school administration was demanding that janitors take them down immediately—it

Figure 1 A survivor speaking with co-founder Kimiya Factory at an anti-Kavanaugh protest on the campus of UTSA (2018). Photo by Dominique Beltran.

was at that very moment that I came to terms with what I was up against. The truth of rape culture.

I remember coming out of the stall after taping up the last of the statements that I had in my trench coat. A janitor was standing right outside the stall that I came out of—we locked eyes and stared at each other for what felt like eternity. I handed her the statement and motioned for her to read it. She read it and glanced back up at me—I pleaded with my eyes and simply stated,

> Please don't take these down this week. This needs to happen.

She nodded and left the restroom. I didn't know it then, but I would run into many people like her, who knew the resistance needed to survive. Solidarity is one of the many necessary

The Daily

Female UTSA Students Come Forward and Protest Against Sexual Assault

by AJ Lopez | November 30, 2018 at 7:45 PM

comment ∨

Figure 2 A screenshot of a newspaper article featuring students at UTSA during a protest (2018). Photo by Dominique Beltran.

ingredients of the revolution. A neutral understanding that for the entire boat to float, the weight needs to be shared. At that moment, I never even needed to know her story—one never needs to know the other's story to co-exist and survive. I hope she's doing well; I hope she reads this. Thank you.

It wasn't more than a week before the flyers took to Twitter and then on November 20, My SA, a local news source, reported on

Living histories: The beginning of #CRC   27

Figure 3 Beginning coverage of the movement. Photo by Dominique Beltran.

them, headline titled, "UTSA President applauds flyers taking stand against 'rampant sexual assault and abuse'".

My blood boiled and seethed, because I knew that the university only applauded the flyers because they couldn't get rid of them. They had no choice but to commend the speaking out of survivors, or else they would have to face the complacency that occurred on their campus with Title IX. But we were nowhere near done yet.

Figure 4 Co-founder Kimiya Factory leading a protest on campus. Photo by Dominique Beltran.

Exercise 2.1: Living history writing exercise 1—personal histories

Objectives: This writing exercise can be used to strengthen participants' connection to personal narratives and storytelling.

Instructions:

1. Tell the learners and facilitators that the following exercise requires extended periods of writing and sharing stories. Please ask them to move to more comfortable positions and/or comfortable people.
2. Next, offer a myriad of participation methods within the activity. Some may choose to participate in silence, virtually, in person, in writing, or not at all. If they ask to leave class please allow them to. Discuss that literature is multimodal

(comes in many different forms) and so will the work. Playlists, menus, photos, art, video, and other forms are encouraged!

3. Prompt listed and unlisted story prompts about any topic surrounding something inherently "personal" to the participants. Write, record, or document in 15-minute intervals. In between writing, encourage students to read their stories to someone or to themselves.
4. If the participants wish to do so, make time before the end to share stories.

Examples of "personal" narrative prompt questions

1. Write, narrate, or document a time in your life you felt you were eating the best thing you had ever tasted.
2. Write, narrate, or document a time in your life when you traveled alone.
3. Write, narrate, or document a notable moment from your childhood.
4. Write, narrate, or document a time in your life you saw something that you do not think anyone else would believe you saw.
5. Write, narrate, or document a time in your life you surprised yourself.
6. Write, narrate, or document a time in your life you had a really good day.
7. Write, narrate, or document a time in your life when you felt like a good friend.

3
Survivor-centered models and a culture of consent

Flashbacks of a comment that I overheard my freshman year of college rang in my ears all day on November 29, 2018, as I organized a protest that would disrupt one of UTSA's annual and expensive events that celebrate the holiday season: the Lighting at the Paseo. "Yeah bro, she texted me this morning that I fucked her so hard that I made her bleed", a football player on UTSA's football team at the time casually bragged as he bumped fists with another one of his teammates at an on-campus hang out I found myself at. I remember hearing that statement in my head every time that I heard his number called and chanted at football games, after that night. I wondered if the girl he bragged about was okay. I wondered if she gave consent. The entire day of November 29, 2018, comments similar to the one I mentioned quelled any second thoughts that I had about the protest later that night. I could barely eat, as I knew that in the evening I would officially be associated with the flyers distributed around campus. Whispers about the manifesto that we released surrounded me in my classes, and social media was swarming with praise for President Eighmy's acknowledgment of the flyers, painting our statement as a mere "cry for help". I knew that it was so much more. The sun set as I made my way to the common area around the corner with a bag full of bullhorns.

The women of UTSA, and others who had heard about the demonstration through the grapevine, all arrived to help handmake posters. Without exchanging a word, I watched everyone write each letter on the posters with a story that I would never ask them to tell. In that moment, I realized how rape culture can even be the burden that accompanies asking someone to share their story or relive their trauma. I learned to only thank someone for their story, because we are never owed it. We all gathered at the stairs of the Paseo, several feet above where the event was being held. The Rowdy Mascot danced and Christmas carols played as I and supporting organizations stared down with absolute determination to be heard.

Before I knew it, my bullhorn raised and I screamed at the top of my lungs, "WE BELIEVE YOU". The group chanted after me. "CHANGE RAPE CULTURE" the crowd chanted as we made our way down the stairs. The music halted and a crowd of people stared, mouths agape, flashlights shining from their camera phones as they created a path. Tears leaked down my cheeks, screaming with everything I ever had in me. The DJ then turned the music up over us, as the administration scrambled to instruct Rowdy, the school mascot, to keep dancing and carry on as usual. We stood and chanted over the music for over an hour while being booed—strobe lights shining on us, as our dignity leaked onto the very campus we worked to pay tuition and be silenced for. I remember the administration making eye contact with me and shaking their heads, as I stared right back and chanted louder.

That was the very first night #ChangeRapeCulture protested. Little did I know that I needed every ounce of strength that night gave me to overcome the backlash that awaited me.

Following the protest at the Lighting of the Paseo, UTSA's Title IX office, UTSA Administration, and Student Affairs all tracked down my email inbox, with generic links to counseling services and pleas to share with them the stories that I heard. I sternly refused, seeing as the survivors' safety was my top priority and, ultimately, because the stories that I was trusted with were never mine to tell. I refused meetings with the university for a cold month, as threats arose from the rapists towards the women of UTSA. Women in the group were discouraged one by one, and soon enough, my co-founder Taylor Waits and I were the only people at the forefront of the movement.

Personally, my life was in shambles. I was suffering from chronic anxiety, finals were in full swing, my family thought that I was on a personal death wish, and media outlets were only interested in our perspective if we were willing to put survivors in further danger by naming campus rapists on air. I remember a reporter who refused to cover the story in depth told me, "Rapes happen everywhere, sweetie. Give us a reason to air this". The casual nature of that statement disgusted me. Rapes and violation of bodily autonomy shouldn't happen to begin with—I felt like I was drowning, and then I would remember how people who are assaulted feel every day. I kept going. Then, on December 19, 2018, a caring and empathetic journalist, dedicated to reporting the truth in the city, ran a front-page headlining story in the *San Antonio Express News* titled "UTSA students' push against 'rape culture' has murky aftermath" (Torraiva, 2018). This two-page story followed my fight from the beginning—and for the first time in a while I felt like I could breathe. This story made me human; it made the movement out to be exactly what it was about—accurate survivor representation and accountability. In many ways, it also was the beginning. I had no idea that, at that moment, I had challenged a statewide institution in front of the seventh largest city in the nation.

Retaliation. I always wondered what the threat of equality and justice really meant when speaking the honest truth about violence and brutality in the history of civil rights. Often wondering what was "radical" about the basic concepts of humanity. The history of rape culture functions to silence the voice of survivors. Constantly working to discourage people from telling their stories at the cost–benefit analysis of not being believed. This is what I realized I was up against. A privilege that I once had but never care to have again—I will always choose to believe. Who knew that a law created to protect the livelihood of individuals in workplaces, schools, and social settings could be the very legal ground that campuses stand on to say that they're doing "enough". Survivors deserve more than enough. We deserve our lives back—our hope in humanity, our belief in the falsehood that universities would protect us.

In the State of Texas, as per Title IX, under the federal civil rights law, schools must protect students from gender-based violence and harassment, including rape and sexual assault. In addition to sexual harassment, this includes harassment on the basis of sex, sex stereotypes, sex characteristics, sexual orientation, gender identity, and pregnancy or parenting status as well as any related conditions—whether or not the harassment is sexual in nature.

A Title IX Coordinator is a person designated by your school district to ensure compliance with Title IX. A Title IX Coordinator's responsibilities include, but are not limited to:

- Investigating reports of sexual harassment, sexual assault, abuse, or other gender-based violence;
- Managing the response to reports and complaints of sexual harassment, sexual assault, abuse, or other gender-based violence; and
- Coordinating the grievance procedure for Title IX complaints.

Professors called me out in classes with snide remarks, my peers stared as I walked on campus, and I even lost some of my closest friends that disagreed with my strategy. But the one thing that I had through it all were the survivors and their testimonies. Strangers would embrace me at every corner I turned, silently whispering a "thank you" with giant tears threatening to leak from their eyes. Three-minute verbal exchanges of brutal rape stories and generational molestation would fill my days. I connected with every soul that I encountered as I took a piece of their trauma and buried it deep inside me. I would imagine exchanging light as I hugged them—a radiance that no rapist could ever take away. I wiped the tears off of countless cheeks as they sometimes wiped tears off of mine, after hearing their story to never see them again. I didn't have to see them again—their story would always be enough for me to keep on fighting.

The university couldn't begin to fathom my bond with survivors on campus as it became more evident that #ChangeRapeCulture was a trusted source. In the first meeting that I agreed to meet with the university, they wasted no time gaslighting me through the mouth of a soft-spoken Black administrator.

"There are other ways to be heard. No need to be so loud". I stared at her in awe, as every story that I heard daily was further validated in the way I was offered to be on committees and boards in a persuasive effort to be less "verbally vocal" and "more diplomatic" about the rapes occurring on campus.

I stood my ground, and shamed every office that dealt with sexual misconduct for asserting that I should do their job for them—even though I already was in an organic, communal context (which is way stronger, in my opinion).

I'll never forget when I finally met with President Taylor Eighmy—he put on his best voice and gave me a flimsy gesture of gratitude while we sat at his expensive mahogany oak wood table. I watched as his hands shook, wondering who had written his script that morning in an effort to handle the "noisy Black girl" who needed to be shut up. I was a problem, and it was written all over his face. He pressed his lips into a tight smile as I met his eyes with a cold, determined gaze.

I gagged at everyone's formality, and counted the seconds that it took for me to reach the several floors at the end of the elevator towards the ivory tower, considering that we were all gathering at the expense of the brutal rape of UTSA's students. I stared right into UTSA President Taylor Eighmy's eyes and reminded him that, with graduation approaching in only one week, he would be shaking the hands of rapists that would walk the stage—with a degree that they would continue to harm others in society with. I then glanced at every suit and tie in the room and reminded them that I wouldn't crack. No amount of false diplomacy would take away my promise to these people's stories and lives—I told them to get to work. Real work. Not the kind that feeds their families with a weekly Google sheet evaluation of workplace culture checkmarks, but REAL WORK. Of hearing me scream through my bullhorn and their praying that every soul who raped a person on their campus could be delivered from the pits of patriarchal hell for their crime of robbing a person of their bodily autonomy.

Christmas break of 2019 was the most soul searching that I thought I ever had to do. Stories that I would hear during the day would keep me up into the night as I would comb over similarities that each and every rape story shared—the soulless look in the eye of the perpetrator as they raped their victims, the luring of girls at parties to be drugged by drug-laced edibles, the flinch of the person telling me their story, the longing in their eyes for me to believe them. I would toss and turn, remembering the rape culture intertwined in college advice at backyard barbeques like "keep up with the pepper spray", followed by a wink. I then had to come to terms with my own abuse and trauma if I was going to fight this fight. I had to understand that surviving had so much strength in itself—surviving the system is something that we all do.

At an event that I was speaking at, a person approached me and kindly corrected me on being called a "victim". She stated, "I'm more than that—what I have been through is more than that. I survive what happened to me every day". I vowed to never put someone or their experience in a box again.

I hope one understands though—I had an amazing network of people who fought silently by supporting me in whatever ways they could. Professors who would see me protesting and forgive my tardiness with a stern nod, attorneys who would advise me pro bono, mentors who would slide me a breakfast taco from their purse because they knew that I was forgetting to eat.

I want so badly to tell her that the act of rape and sexual assault happen outside of college campuses. Ultimately she's more exhausted from this devastating truth that I have told her.

I would tell her that we are protected by angels. Angels who were ordained by the ancestors to remind me that I was never alone—that I was fighting a fight that came generations before I even existed.

Ordained angels—if you're reading this, I don't even think the depths of the ocean could measure up to my love and gratitude for you. Thank you for lifting me up; oftentimes I would hope that my tired smile was gratitude enough. But you knew the risk of this college girl subject to ridicule and criticism—convinced that she could help change the world. And you didn't care. You sat next to me, walked me to my car, stood up for me when I wasn't in the room, and gave me a gentle nod when I would spy you in the crowd at protests. You would hand me the tape to hang up a call-to-action, or edit footage for social media. You would tuck a stone in the palm of my hand or offer me a cold bottle of water while I was sweating and chanting in the sun. It would all add up to building a sturdy foundation that I found to be my back—with the life-changing weight of many strong souls to carry. Sweating, seething with everything to lose—but also everything to gain.

4
Living histories
Strategy and survival

Shymrri's story

I guess I really am as vain as my maw maw usually spat out loud whenever she caught me admiring my appearance for longer than a second.

I never told Maw Maw how these moments are fleeting and tomorrow I'll go back to my normal routine of self-loathing. I never told Maw Maw of the cuts buried into my wrist under my clothing. I let her think of me as the most vain little girl. I plunged my open wound bravely into the dishwater **with a tablespoon of bleach**, careful that my new mother didn't find me useless.

I sometimes wonder what it was like to grow up as one of the "dark-skin sisters" while surrounded by the "High Yeller" sisters her father had gifted with his redbone. I wonder often what it was like for Maw Maw. What experiences could have shaped her into the old lady in front of me? After all, this was her first time being an old lady too.

The resignation of a long-lived life sits behind Maw Maw's eyes now. Her eyes are warm and tired brown. Like, if you had seen what they saw you'd be tired too. She speaks of the fact that I will miss her when she is gone and think of all those things that old lady said. She speaks of herself in the third person. **I wonder if Maw Maw knows she is vain too.**

I don't tell Maw Maw that I've been grieving her since I learned what death did to Grandmas and Papas. That I've fought off the dark thoughts and held her close to my heart. I don't tell Maw Maw that I already miss her out of fear that it will make her sad. I don't tell Maw Maw I've used up all of my love on her and how she has both overflowed and emptied me. I buy her flowers instead because an old person once said,

"Buy my flowers while I am still here".

So I buy her flowers, the same ones I'll place on her casket, I presume.

I wonder what Maw Maw would think of the Bible I bought today. I could have told her earlier on the phone. Maybe somewhere in the pages I'll find the forgiving father that she speaks of all the time. The man who stole my Sundays and lurked around the corners of late Saturday nights. Like there wasn't really a Friday because there was Saturday morning cleaning to wake for. Of course, there wasn't really a Sunday because that day belonged to White God and that night belonged to preparing for Monday morning school.

When Maw Maw calls and asks me about school and my books, I do not tell her how hard college is. No, I just let her live through me. I let her teenage Harlem dreams flourish through my fingertips as I type out all of my lil essays, big ideas. I do not think of the lurking deadlines and mental health episodes. I do not let the fear of a fast approaching adulthood without her bother me. Instead, I tell her of the peaceful walks to the cafe and my English teacher's interest in me. I tell her what he said about my writings, and she tells me of hers. They were all lost in Hurricane Katrina, you see, so I'll never get to read them. And I think it is such a tragedy, a life where writing goes to waste. So I tell her about days at the G and promise her Grambling Mom T-shirts. In exchange she tells me of the white women who spat at her. You see, she lives through me and I feel through her. Two generations living side by side, the fight and the peace and the new fight of course all within thee.

I suppose I am just as vain as she's cursed me to be. Like, put this perm in your hair so you'll be less of a **nigger**, you see. I do not tell Maw Maw that she cannot burn whiteness into me.

I let her try.

I do write all of these pieces of writing about us. I talk constantly about myself. Trauma looks much better when decorated with pretty words. My life isn't the worst in particular, just a well-told story. I dream of blue magic grease, a hot comb and Naami. We sit on the front porch after Katrina has washed away everything that was. Washed away my two sisters and I into a new family with new last names embroidered into old country belts. See, all I had ever known was Shymrri McDonald but they had memories of what it was like to be another. I think often of the lazy days spent on that old country porch. I think of the beaming sun and the white little curly-haired puppy racing across the big front yard. I think of how Solo won't be a puppy forever and that I cannot wish life into him. I think of his brief time with the new white puppy and how Angel must have felt when he disappeared. I think of the two white puppies hovering in the sky above me. I often think of Angel and Solo as I think of me and Naami. A given love. The kind you just sort of sat back and received. Before the world taught us to hate we were all just made of love, you see. We were made of Mama Noodles and the burn on my sister's thigh. You see, Kehnemah was my rock. My sister, my protector, my mother in ways unknown to my pea-sized brain. I lived in the cuts she never thought I saw, and the cries where I held her without knowing what for. You see, I am my sister's keeper, and they are allowed to use me. To cry here on this shoulder any time for free. They have gained my trust and in me live the three of us guarded by white puppies with new wings.

I want to go to my older sister's baby girl and get on one knee and say, "Here's Kabot, you see, he protected us and now he will protect you".

I will hand her the old brown teddy bear that came from my first sister Tahzri, then onto the hand of Kehnemah and Naami.

I reckon one day, **when it is too late**, I'll sit down with Maw Maw and tell her to tell me it all, and I reckon that's why I haven't written my first book. I reckon I'll write of my Maw Maw and what it was like to know her.

I suppose I'll smile and dance, I'll shake my unrhythmic hips to her Harlem dreams, like she'd say

"I never dreamed of Harlem daughter, that was for the rich gals and daddy had eight kids, you see".

She'd tell me of how useless American **negro-stained blood** dreams were when you was just some Black girl growing up in Mississippi.

I think of my upbringing, of my **some Black girl growing up in Louisiana**, that wasn't much better odds than what she had, but it was, just a little bit, better. I think people often grow content with where we as a negro race are. They don't see how little it is that we leaped. I think I can, of course, because I can see it through Maw Maw as she can see it through me, like one of us looking into the past and the other into the future. We notice we haven't taken a whole lot of steps.

I think of my upbringing and my childhood spent at Moton. A school that just couldn't seem to be still the whole while I was there. Every year there would be a new building but the same people. I guess this is why I bleed my creative blood onto every corner in New Orleans; I guess, you see, that is why this city is rooted in me. While it is hurricane-cursed but can never wash me away.

I think of the infamous Mr Baptiste and his collection of my books during math class. I'd plead with the bald-headed Black man for my escape into fantasy. You see the doctor had said I had ADHD and I did much better when my hyperfixation was trapped in a book, you see. The more books he'd take from me the more I'd be inspired to make. When I wasn't reading I was writing, and I had found the never-ending cycle I am trapped in still to this day. I'd dreamingly stapled short stories made of notebook paper and passed them around the classroom. I told them to read my book, you see.

I wonder what that first slave thought, all those years ago, when he realized that he, too, could read the white man's word.

I often think of Sundays spent in those wretched blue pews but Maw Maw was happy with her big hat so I suppose that I could sit or sleep for a little while. I remember how she struggled with her words when reading the Bible.

I remember my mocking gaze and correction of her words.

I remember the old lady next to us who said, "Do not correct your elders, they are rarely wrong, you see". I think of how she was supposed to bake me a cake for my 16th birthday but died before. I think of all the funerals I went to with Maw Maw. **All the funerals.**

I never cried for her. I think I will cry now, while I write and properly grieve the lady who brought me notebooks and pens, and allow myself to remember that this is where it truly began … right. Where I wrote my first stories. I think of all the people, all the characters in my life who have come and gone. Like who was real and who was fake. I am an unreliable narrator, you see. I cannot tell you what's a story and what's real life, and what is the difference anyway? We are all stories …

But you see, Maw Maw wore really big hats.

Figure 5 Shymrri outside the apothecary in New Orleans, LA. Photo by Taylor Waits.

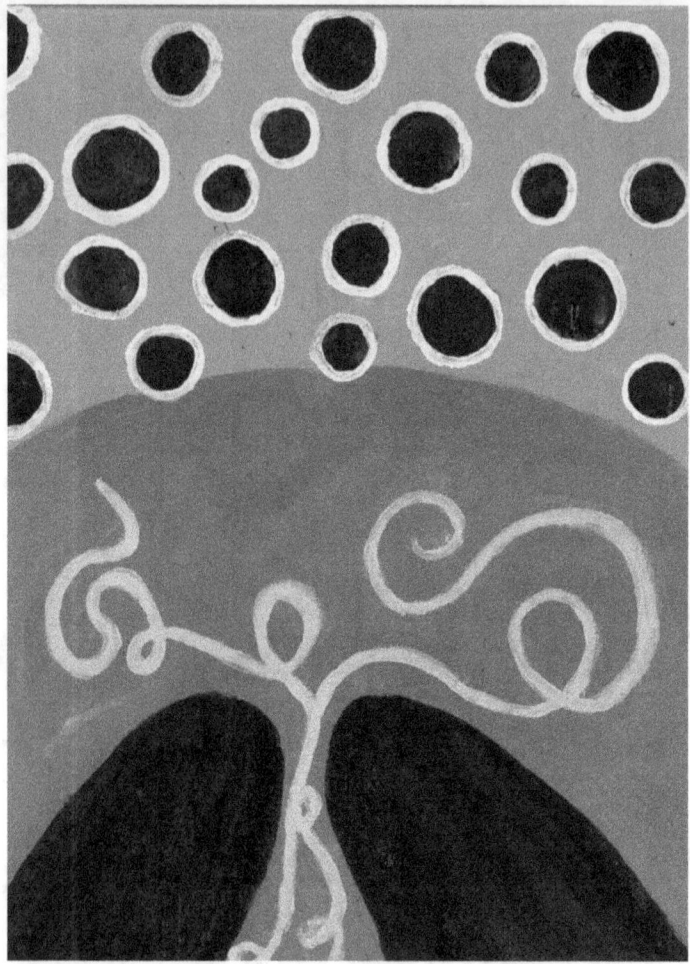

Figure 6 Untitled. A human re-teaching my body, my mind, and my world who I am. I love y'all. Coreen Monique.

Shymrri McDonald is a sophomore journalism student at Grambling University. She writes about her childhood growing up in New Orleans, Louisiana; her experience as a survivor; and other musings.

Taylor's story

In 2019, we had reached a turning point. Should we continue to grow #CRC or archive what we'd done and hope for the best. Kimiya was finishing her last year of undergrad down in Texas and I was beginning my PhD program in Pittsburgh. The momentum that #ChangeRapeCulture had grown in a year fruited a bustling social media page, a few mini documentaries, and a handful of media appearances. Our university was in the works of deconstructing the Title IX office. We had a hopeful following of survivors on and off campus since #CRC started. It was miraculous. However, regardless of the success of our movement, Kimiya and I could not escape the cycle of violence that is abuse. Several of our key familial relationships began to deteriorate. We both were running low on energy and capacity. And to add to the chaos, several white feminists had tried to overtake the movement. Despite the circumstances we decided to see where #CRC went for the year. We relied heavily on *The Combahee River Collective Statement* (The Combahee River Colletive, 1977) for guidance on what to do next. These feminists speak of infighting due to homophobia, transphobia, racism, and colorism being the root causes of their inability to meet together and have actions. They detail feelings of frustration, wasted time, misunderstanding, and hopelessness. They ask for the readers and society at large to focus resources specifically on those most marginalized in our societies, specifically Black women (cis, trans, and gender non-conforming). So the question running through our minds became: Are we centering ourselves in how we run this movement? If we tire ourselves out it will just dissolve. But what about the rest of the survivors? All those stories we heard on campus? What if we really try to grow our movement? What *could* happen next?

During the times in a Black person's life that we want to protect our natural hair instead of wearing it out, we employ a protective hairstyle. However, before a protective style can be worn, a foundation must be set. Like for other Black folks who prioritize their hair, the attention to detail and specific measures taken in order to protect the hair vary from head to head. However, the idea of wearing a "protective style" is almost synonymous with Black experience across the globe. The idea is to protect all hair growth already made while encouraging more growth. The hair is braided down into cornrows after being saturated with products that keep its shine, encourage growth, and repair frayed or damaged hair. The scalp is then revealed, giving the person the flexibility to receive moisture and have the moisture sealed. This process is repeated throughout the hair's duration in this protective style. While in this protected style the wearer can now experiment with hairstyles while keeping their braids in.

After a whirlwind of a year filled with threats, media coverage, on-campus drama, and vacuous emails from university administrators, **#ChangeRapeCulture needed a protective style.** We started this movement with all guns a-blazing. We had been wearing our hair out all year and our ends started looking thin and scraggly. We deprioritized our own health for the sake of keeping up momentum. Our cracks were beginning to show. When folks would ask us what we did or who we were, we no longer felt right saying we were "just a student movement". Our words and ideas had long stretched past our university. We had been asked to speak at conferences in California, Texas,

Pennsylvania, and Louisiana. #CRC had made appearances on CNN, in newspapers across the nation, and our email was flooded with other survivors wanting to connect. After a year, we finally felt like **now** we can breathe. Assess. Decide if this was what we wanted to do.

After a few weeks of rest and deliberation we each decided to move forward in making #CRC a 501(c)(3) organization. While we both detest the industrial complex that is non-profitism we knew we needed a way to secure more money for more survivors. We decided that #CRC was bigger than Kimiya and me. The world needs #ChangeRapeCulture whether we are a part of it or not. Queer and/or survivors of color need specific resources. They need to be prioritized in holistic care models. And they need to continue to have their stories elevated. In 2020 we were going to attempt to put CRC's cornrows in.

We wanted to spend 2020 achieving three goals:

1. **Building programming for survivors by survivors;**
2. **Protecting our community from backlash; and**
3. **Spreading anti-rape culture rhetoric as far and wide as possible.**

On February 6, 2020, we expanded our movement from the @changerapeculturetx page to our @chngerpecltre main page. That same day we re-launched our websites and social media pages, and announced our staff—Kimiya and me. Then we went to work. With the COVID-19 pandemic preventing us from hosting any in-person events we were forced to come up with new and innovative ways to empower queer and/or BIPOC survivors. We hosted online art galleries and Instagram

Figure 7 Co-founder Taylor Waits participating in the Queer and Trans Survivors Play Day in 2020. Photo by DirectedByYash.

Figure 8 Altar Piece by Takara Canty for Kimiya's Ball in 2021. Photo by DirectedByYash.

live talks, created a sex worker resource page, started a chapter in Pittsburgh, hosted two drag shows for Black women, raised money for our 501(c)(3) establishment, started the #OPENYOURPURSE mutual aid fundraiser, opened our #CRCAmbassadors youth group, started selling merchandise, and started our #SetYourselfFree support groups. In one year we had collaborated with ten community partners to service survivors. And that was with just two employees. We ended 2020 utterly exhausted and with almost zero funding. We hadn't received as many donations as we initially thought and ended up paying for a year's worth of programming fully out of pocket. Despite taking so many months to raise money for our 501(c)(3) formation we still fell short when needing to establish an LLC formation beforehand (which also costs money). Mixed with the racism of the banking system and IRS we were stuck on how to move forward. I was going hungry in Pittsburgh and lying to Kimiya about how expensive things

Figure 9 Participants at Kimiya's Ball: A Celebration for Black Women in Pittsburgh in 2021. Photo by DirectedByYash.

were to keep everything maintained. My mental health began slipping and our programming was beginning to slip because of it. We were on such a roll. I didn't want it to be because of me that we lost it all. Our cornrows were laid but we had not prepared our hair first. The style looked pristine from the outside, but a closer look at the scalp will show irritation and dryness. We would have to take out the braids and start again. This time we would stand on our values. This time would be different.

During this time in 2021 I found myself going back to the writings that helped us establish our movement. I would read *A Black Feminist Statement* by the Combahee River Collective every day. Specifically, the portion that denounces queenhood and martyrdom. I was tired of Kimiya and I feeling like our experiences were singular and like our issues weren't community issues. We came from the idea that we all must share in the suffering of survivors until we are all prioritizing creating a safer world for them. Systems are built and maintained by people. Two queer Black women screaming anti-rape culture rhetoric at folks is only one way to #ChangeRapeCulture—but not the only way. We were tired of having all the responsibility fall to us and wanted to ensure that our programming would never be dependent on another human being again. #CRC is about community—until we had the team needed to sustain #CRC we were going to have to do less. We needed #CRC to run itself, 501(c)(3) status or not.

At the top of 2021, Kimiya and I met again and decided to work smarter and not harder. We were going to communicate more but work less. We were going to maintain the events we could and establish communicable ways to teach any and everyone how to host supportive events for survivors. The more folks that want to #ChangeRapeCulture the better! We began accepting volunteers who helped us table at events and helped us create relationships with the community, and encouraged survivors to start regularly attending our online and in-person events. Next, we started to reach out to our community for new logos, new merch, new events, and new media to spread. We created mini Instagram posts that promoted anti-rape culture. We hosted events that directly served our survivors like resource fairs, balls, art exhibitions, healing circles, support groups, movie nights, and collaborative art therapy classes. We had continued to center our work around our survivors and through that we grew—exponentially. We have now expanded to four states: Texas, Ohio, Pennsylvania, and Louisiana. We are running programs through all of them with intentions of growing our programs there too. Our fiscal sponsor, Hugh Lane Wellness Foundation, walked us through the process of acquiring the 501(c)(3) and offered us monetary and education support to finally achieve our status by the end of 2022. We have added a new community member, Coreen, into our New Orleans team. We now offer exclusive blog submissions to spread rhetoric from survivors about rape culture. We started making more of a social media presence on Twitter and TikTok. And we are finishing our formative documents to prepare us for our filing with the IRS. We look forward to hiring a financial advisor and grant writer who will allow us to rely less on our community for money and more on federal and state funding. We were surviving but now we work on thriving.

Exercise 4.1: Living history writing exercise 2—group histories

Objectives: This writing exercise can be used to strengthen participants' connection to personal narratives, group histories, and storytelling.

Instructions:

1. Tell the learners and facilitators that the following exercise requires extended periods of writing and sharing stories. Please ask them to move to more comfortable positions and/or comfortable people.
2. Next, offer a myriad of participation methods within the activity. Some may choose to participate in silence, virtually, in person, in writing, or not at all. If they ask to leave class please allow them to. Discuss that literature is multimodal (comes in many different forms) and so will the work. Playlists, menus, photos, art, video, and other forms are encouraged!
3. Have participants decide whether or not they will create small group narratives or one narrative by the entire group.
4. Prompt listed and unlisted story prompts about any topic surrounding something inherently "group" to the participants. Write, record, or document the beginning, middle, and end of the narrative.
5. If the participants wish to do so, make time before the end to share stories.

Examples of "group" narrative prompt topics:

1. Re-telling of campus community current events;
2. Re-telling of class or facilitation time; and
3. Summary of cultural events occurring at the time.

5
How to advocate for university student survivors—podcast transcription

On July 23, 2023, Coreen Hale and Taylor Waits recorded a podcast detailing their personal experience with rape culture on campus via Zoom. This conversation centers around three central questions marked in bold lettering followed by the respondents' answers in real time. Within this conversation they discuss how to be an advocate for student survivors, talk about community accountability, and offer advice to those seeking help.

1. Can you tell me about a time you were confronted with rape culture in college?

    Coreen H.: Okay. I would say definitely a time, not the first time … it wasn't the last time that I experienced rape culture on campus. I had an experience where I perpetuated rape culture within my friend group. It came from a lack of understanding, a lack of knowing, you know, just a lot of a lot, a lot of assumptions. And it was one of the things like when I understood where rape culture was. I realized that I was a perpetuator of it, like very directly to a man. It was kind of one of the most difficult things for me to grapple with, especially being a person that had been sexually assaulted as a child, and like as a young adult, knowing that I had also perpetuated that on somebody was very, very hard, so. But it was us at the end of the day, and for me, because I have a very good circle around me that made sure I did not go unchecked. This is like the next day, right? Because it was the situation where I made two people very uncomfortable. And so within my friend group I received a hard sitting down and a hard talking to, and it made me realize a lot of things about the power that I hold as a woman, and being like a highly sexual woman. I'm open about my sexuality and the things that I like to want and know. I'm going to check that and turn it off, and when it's not like when you're crossing a boundary, and what you may think of as like a part of your identity. Right? And what it really is. It's like not a personality trait, and more than just something you picked up in culture. Okay, you need to stop doing it. And so that was one of the most prominent times like one of the like I think about like my experience with rape culture, all campus in college that's like the shine and be in the light that I think about. Yeah.

Taylor W.: I think for me there's been lots of times that I perpetuated rape culture with lots of different people. And that's the radicalness of changing rape culture and not ending it. It is the idea that everybody is perpetuating it, and that there is no like—(Taylor gets sidetracked)—obviously sexually assaulting someone is fucked up, and that's not going to be as bad as like stealing a cracker from a store. But how we see it is whether you were in my circumstance where you're a bystander, and you don't do anything or you are perpetuating assault you are both just as bad. I'm kind of going into the second question, but we know that it's really hard for men to come forward with their stories especially with trans men. With Black people coming forward with their stories especially when you are in a community. And so that was the point that I was in where I wasn't stepping up and being the friend that's holding this person accountable, right? I was really close friends to several people who were in abusive relationships and were in the cycle of violence. And instead of speaking up and protecting these people or telling the people that they were in these relationships with like, "Hey, I don't really like the way you treat these people", or "I don't like the way that you talk to them", or "I don't like the way you talk to me". I kept it the same way I always deal with things. That's their business, and that's their relationship. And then because we failed to address the elephants in the room these people would bring me in and put me in their relationships. They would have me slicing tires with them, or, you know, going place to place to terrorize people. So, I'm with you in the fact of perpetuating the exact thing that we said we weren't going to do. That's what we want for everybody with ChangeRapeCulture is to realize, how are you a perpetuator in the system, and how can you help or advocate in your specific perspective? How can your friends, how can we, as a community, hold people accountable to what has happened in a way to move forward. A lot of things that people ask us as like, well, what about the abuser? What about them? And it's not about that, as you said, with being sat down with being spoken to, with being addressed like, it's not about walking on eggshells around this person. It's about keeping the survivor safe. So, you know, I have really complicated relationships to a lot of those people. Now. I would say that I've lost like genuine time and energy to violence, because it's similar with racism. It takes up so much of your time that you're so busy trying to walk on eggshells around this person or around your friend's boyfriend or around, you know, your friends, partner, your friends, whoever your friend's girlfriend. That you don't really get to spend the time that you wish that you had. So, looking back in college on these like inherently amazing moments. Sometimes they're really soured by how rampant rape, abuse, you know, just taking advantage of people was at that time and in society. Now it's not just on college campuses, it's everywhere. So as you said that wasn't my first time or my last time. And it probably, you know, was one of many times that I just was not enough, that I did not do enough, that I did not stand up enough. I didn't speak up enough. I didn't read enough. And that was when I had to confront myself. Well, how am I doing these things? What do I think about rape culture? What do I think about this? Especially coming from being assaulted myself. You can look up the statistics as to how close it is to people who perpetuate violence and those who have also been sexually assaulted or who have come from homes that perpetuate violence. You could see that they're intrinsically connected. There's obviously nuance to that. But we know that when we were traumatized in these sacred and intimate moments, whether your first assault is while you're on campus or before then, you're going to have a very skewed view as to what is normal. A lot of my survivor friends will say like what I do in my house is normal to me. You know one of my friends who has somebody in their family molesting them they thought that was normal. This is normal. So when you make jokes, when you proceed to have these skeemy encounters with people, and they tell you it isn't normal you feel alone.

Coreen H.: Yeah! College is a weird place to be, because so many people from so many different places are coming together. I think some of us are in positions where we're in a mishmash of people who a lot of times have had similar experiences to us. We just kind of like bounce off of one another to create a really toxic environment. There are rapes happening. I think a part of it is knowing that college campuses are places where like individual work can be done but because there's that opportunity for people to just agree with you—you don't question your actions. Either we are going to bounce off each other and recreate all the things that we've been experiencing and not questioning what's going on, or we could like come together with all these differences in shit like that, and just actually sit down and be like, "Hey. I think it's weird that we're all doing this. I think it's weird that we all accept this. So I think it's weird that, you know, we all move this way, even though it makes us uncomfortable, even though we all don't fucking lie here. But we still do it". College campus is a not a good place to make that realization. It's not. It's not the best place. It's a hard place for it [rape] to happen.

2. What are some obstacles to serving queer and of-color survivors?

Taylor W.: Yeah, that goes amazingly into the second question. I know my experience from serving survivors of color, specifically queer survivors of color as well as queer survivors, and survivors of color who aren't queer, and I know from my own experience that your culture has a lot to do with how you react to sexual violence and how you were raised. You know your childhood is who you are now, and I think a lot of us obviously have to come to heads with that, and for me, specifically, I was raised as a Black American to be a woman and to provide, you know I would say, structure to a home, and I was brought up as a Christian. And my parents were very strict, so I was brought up to think that, you know, I'm going to marry a man. I'm going to serve him. We're going to serve Jesus, God, and we're going to build this life around these ideals, right? And when you grow up in a patriarchal, you know, homophobic, transphobic household, already you're holding that like you said and go into this environment with all these people aka college. And then, you know, being radicalized into thinking, "Maybe this isn't right?" So, um, there's already obstacles. I really hate it when people have this innocent survivor take or the perfect victim trope. That survivors do no wrong or have to be in a perfect circumstance to excuse the abuse.

Coreen H.: That's because it makes people less likely to talk about their trauma and the survivorship, because they think if I'm not the perfect survivor, then I'm not really one. Am I right?

Taylor W.: Yeah, we had these moments where we were sexually assaulted as children. And then, you know, you kind of have that time one of my really amazing writer friends Lexi Bean consistently says, people are always asking them, was it the assault that made you trans, or were you trans before the assault? Were you queer because of this? Are you this way because of the assault? It's like yes and no right like, of course, as a queer person the experiences that happen to me, especially the deeply traumatic ones, are going to alter the way that I think. But that's not the one answer, or the one nuanced way of being queer, thus bringing me to transness. Right? So a lot of people will gaslight you out of being a survivor and your survivorship, and the way that you move through your survivorship because it's like, well, you don't really even know who you are or you don't know because you're queer. Is it normal? You need to figure out what you want that's normal, because that's—being queer—already not normal. Then the second portion of that, as well as being of color, is just not having access to correct accurate resources that are also spoken in a way that are accessible. Being a Black American, there are thousands of people that I know of all races who has assaulted somebody during sex, unknowingly, because they just simply didn't know that stealthing or having sex with somebody who's past a certain limit, or doing all of these other exploring things, or they might hear it in a song. Well, you know, we hear that people are getting, you know, roofied, that people are doing really wild things on drugs and not remembering what's happening and it's reinforced on social media. That's like the whole point of the sex act a lot of my survivors that I work with assumed. They talk about things like,

"Well, it's, you know, that's what people want, I thought that's what you wanted."

Coreen H.: Yup, something we're supposed to do.

Taylor W.: You know, we're taught to act all these ways. How am I supposed to know which one's right and which one's wrong? The third part is like accountability, right? It's hard to be held accountable when you don't know what is right and wrong. And when you don't have access to a therapist, when you don't have access to comparable mental health care. When you don't have access to medication or just holistic ways to keep yourself together, for me one of my medications is marijuana, you know. If it's illegal in your state then you're not going to have access to that as well as being a, you know, a young adult. You're under the age of 21. You're also going to be barred from so many other things, unless you're a non-traditional student and shout out to non-traditional students. But the obstacles really just come from continuously not being believed. Both being a woman and being Black as well as being gay. And you know this is what I'm hearing from other queer and of-color people, specifically, survivors that we work with. As well as knowing that the institution you go to doesn't care. There's an air of like, nothing's gonna happen. So, you know, that's the second biggest one. Or if you're a queer person, a lot of queer people and people of color do not like cops for very …look up, YouTube, and you can figure out what those reasons might be. So when you don't go to the people who are supposed to help you, or when an institution that's supposed to help you—Title IX, the police, the hospitals, psychiatric wards are supposed to be, and they're not doing that, then why would I even bring this up? Why, I don't want to be held accountable by people who also don't know what's right and what's wrong. You know, we're all on the same level here. And so the biggest obstacle is just like, you know, trying to find peace and trying to find joy and trying to find ways to move forward. Even now we struggle with that. We have a support group that we've been going to for like almost three and a half years and I think we consistently find ourselves like, you know, I love talking to you all, but what are our hopes? What I dream of at night, when I see myself as a person. When is that? I thought, that's what my 19- to 22-year stage is really about. And so something that Shymrri, someone who else is, you know, featured in this book says a lot is like she as a young person, you know, she's 19, are not told the truth like they have asked. You know, her teacher will tell her to apply for college, and she will ask them straight up, "Did you think you're going to be a teacher when you went to college? Did you expect to be making this money? Did you expect you know your family to turn out the way that it did?" And why can't we be honest and say no, that none of us knew anything. None of us know what's going on, really, until it happens. Eighteen-year-olds don't need to be choosing what they're doing immediately, and then getting into debt over that, maybe that structure in and of itself is the weird thing, right? And that's what rape culture does. That's what white normativity does. It just keeps itself at the center, like everyone's always trying to get to that point of whiteness or really peace, safety, financial stability. That emulates being white, that emulates being white and rich and privileged. And yeah, what's the biggest problem? Racism.

Coreen H.: I mean, It's even hard. It's not hard to touch on it. But you touch on this topic so well so eloquently, then I'm sitting here like writing stuff down like yes, that is fucking right. But, I would say that what you said when we were talking about that first question is one of, I think one of the harder obstacles is serving my queer minority. Anyone who's on the outskirts serving them is the idea of their business, and you were talking about it in a relationship to your friends and being a bystander, but thinking about it as their business. But all of us live in those microcosms where we see our business, their business, and there's a point in time when you just have to take on responsibility for the world that you live in, right. Like we all in these microcosms of relationships and things like that. And there's a time when you just gotta say fuck it. Their challenge is my challenge, my challenges, their challenge. And we are not going to continue on saying whose problem is who, you know what I'm saying? And we're all going to hold ourselves accountable today. And that's another part of being on this journey with ChangeRapeCulture with you and with our friends, like it's just changing their mindset of thinking about like being so one-sided. Just me, my person. And I think there's a lot of us. I say about it like this, like normative thinking of like being a sole person like, I'm a sole survivor. I have to take care of myself.

Taylor W.: Oh! This is the colonization tactic most definitely.

Coreen H.: Yes, and it's, you know, it's one of the things that's focused on the most, especially when we talking about rape. And when we're talking about rape culture, because it's the thing that kept our people silent. It's the thing that kept our grandmothers silent. And you know it's going to hold us down if we don't get a grip and realize that is who is going to hold us accountable? You know what I'm saying, who's going to hold each other up? But this is going to support the healing.

Taylor W.: Yeah, well I agree. Individualism is very Western thinking. Of course, it's an imperialist and colonization thing to like think, "We're gonna go over here and tell these inherently communal people like stop caring about what everyone else is feeling and just care about you". So it's an act of revolution to say, like we are going to give a fuck about everybody, and it's really hard, right? Like giving a fuck about ourselves is hard. So how is it that we can then push, you know, other people to think about survivors. And I mean the other way around thinking about survivors as perfect. So how is it that we can then push to think about the community, right? There is this group that my friend always details that there's a space for everybody. Right? There's well it's an incest group, and they have a psychiatrist or a counselor, somebody who's experienced at all levels. You know, there's people who have it happen to them. There's the family members who didn't do anything about it. They either knew or didn't know. There are the perpetuators, obviously, some of which were children. Some of which were adults. And we can see in society the way that we deal with anybody who's deviant. And it's usually with very minimal punishment and just society kind of throwing its hands up and saying, "That person is a weirdo. They're just gonna assault and we don't care how many times they assault. You know these people have vulnerable populations around them when they get caught. We're just gonna throw them in jail". And then, you know there's like I said, those groups. Now, those groups don't all meet at the same time in the same area. Obviously, everybody needs their own space. But it's the idea that it doesn't stop with this one person who was abused. Yes, they are the one who needs the most help. But like you said, the world is rocked because this was allowed to happen. This was able to happen. It gets more nuanced. Obviously, when you get into psychiatry and every single case that we deal with, but every single experience of violence, whether it is all the way up to sexual assault or something that's domestic violence, psychological violence, emotional abuse like you said, making people uncomfortable, like all of those things are things that we need to grow to confront better. And if we don't confront those things we're not going to be able to get to the big stuff, like you said. If three generations of women can go by not even talking to me about sex, like what does that say to us as a society, as a family, like? What is that? What does that really mean? And then how much pressure? I love that you and I are our educators, because how much pressure that leaves to the staff, faculty, everybody to raise your children to raise our children to raise generations of children. Jesus! And we know already we can't do it.

Coreen H.: But imagine how beautiful it would be if we could be on one accord. If parents could work with teachers to work with, you know, aunties and uncles correctly extended family members to say that, like these are the things that we can work on and get better with as a group, you know, as a community. And these other things that we can stand for. I guess the big deal they plan when you segment people and fragment them from one another. That's when this thing starts to fester and fester and become like very, very tragic problems that we now have in this society.

3. What were/are some ways to be an advocate for survivors on campus?

Coreen H.: Best ways to be an advocate, I think is to check yourselves, check in with yourself, see where you are, realize your identity, check in with those thoughts, like those things that you're doing within and the everyday work. Work hard to be open to building community around you, because if you don't have people around you that's also watching you and watching your back and checking you too then, I mean, you're likely to spin out of control. So, you know, having those bonds. So it comes with checking oneself having bonds. Speak up. I think one of the things I'm most grateful for is people who are willing to speak up to me like I'll never forget the conversation that I had with my friend. And did it hurt? Did it make me feel like shit? Absolutely! Did I need to feel like shit? Absolutely! So speaking up even when it may hurt. It probably didn't feel good for her to have to talk to me about that, either. Say those things to me, either, and I'm grateful for her strength in that moment. You know what I'm saying, and so I'm grateful for her being one of those people that's not going to say that's just her business. And she was able to open her mouth and talk to me, and not stand by and stand against the culture of silence in that way. A lot of things that you see everyday on your campus. You and Kimiya can say it best that it only took two people coming together. And look at what you all have created from it. And so looking around you and see where those opportunities are, and listening to the fucking people around you, and believing them the first time are, I will say, some ways to be an advocate, and there are plenty, plenty more. But those are mine.

Taylor W.: Yeah, I love it. I feel like that's like the starting point. It's like social media where people say, "It's free to like this. It's free to share this". And you know all of these things are free. Sticking up for people is free. I know that it was just like a lightbulb change, you know, I had seen, especially in college, you know, there were many a party where people were just having sex next to me, or by my head, or by me, or visually. I could just see it. And in that moment that should have been when I said, like, this is weird, we need to bring this up. Why do we feel like this is okay to be doing this and like you said, knowing the hundreds, maybe even thousands of times that I've been one of those people that I've done that. I have also been one of those people where someone comes to me with a story, and not only do I, I do believe them the first time, but I just immediately tell them I don't know how to help you, and I don't know what to do about that. Like you said, I often project onto other people how I feel about myself as a survivor, which is a lot of shame, a lot of guilt. And I just tell people to bottle it up and leave it alone. You know that would be before 2019, just feeling the same way about myself, and, like you said, it was an inner check in. It's really what I want, especially before I move into the space of advocating for people. Can I say that I'm really an advocate for myself? So that's the first for yourself, baby, as Coreen has said, check in. But advocating for yourself is not just checking in with your mind space. It's also checking in with who you are. As a person. I often ask my survivors, what do you visualize for your life? What does that look like? Some of us are married to our abusers, some of us have babies with our abusers, some of our abusers are our parents and you can't cut certain people out of your life even when you want to. That might be the hardest. I don't want to. My abusers were my parents. They never sexually assaulted me, but they did a bunch of other stuff. And as much as I never want to speak to the one that I do speak to ever again, I want to hold all of that stuff against her. I know for me personally that I want a parent. I want somebody who's going to be a part of my life for the rest of my life. I want to be able to take care of her. I want all of that, and I'm not going to be able to do that if I'm not willing to forgive her. So I had to ask myself, am I going to forgive her? Is she willing to do the work to be forgiven? She was, thankfully. That's hard, and people are willing to do that for themselves. So how can you do that for somebody else? Now it's so easy for me to see that somebody else is going through something, and for me to be able to discern this is their business. But my job as an advocate for these people is to tell them the truth. So when you hear someone's story, it is not your job to poke in as to whether they should be with this person, asking them for retaliation, shout out to all my baddies that go slash tires and beat people up, because that's me. You know and being quick to those things instead. It's like you said, listening. And a lot of times what Kimiya and I have learned is these survivors need friends. They need community. They need people telling them that we can rise above this, and we need people to fight against their abusers. I wish anybody would have reprimanded somebody like your friend. There was nobody that said anything to these abusers but us [Kimiya Factory and Taylor Waits], and that only allowed us to hit the surface of all the survivors. We detail in the book that we had people of color and queer people who were detailing what was happening to them in basically entirely different worlds on campus. We're not going to tackle this pandemic of cis people getting raped and abused, like just going through cis women and men even within the inappropriate faculty and student or faculty and faculty relationships. You're not even touching the surface. You're not at all right. We also detail in the textbook that less than 3 per cent of all sexual assaults are reported, less than 3 per cent are reported, less than 3 per cent. That means 97 per cent of people that have been sexually abused won't tell anybody. They won't tell their Grandma. They won't tell you. They won't tell their pet.

Coreen H.: They might just tell themselves they might never even come to terms that even some people don't even tell them, right. Thank you, because some people don't even admit it to themselves that it happened, that it has happened, that they're ready to take that step forward.

Taylor W.: I understand that that's not your place. You're not their therapist. No, that's not your job. Your job is to not butt yourselves into everybody's life and to force them to make right decisions. But when someone tells me, "I feel like I'm walking on eggshells around this person". Or, "Hey, this instance happened to me, and I think that that's very strange", and you yourself are registering it as abuse after you've looked it up. What are some things that happen in abusive relationships? What do these look like? All I say is, share those resources with that person!

Coreen H.: Let them know.

Taylor W.: Say, "Oh, I don't know anything about that, but I know ChangeRapeCulture has this survivor group that is on Zoom, and I feel like if you go and talk to them", and continue to share the resources. That would be really like you go with them to the website or send them to our Instagram. Just send them on the website, like you don't have to be this savior, and that's what we don't want. We actually go against martyrdom. We do not like trophies. And we do not like this idea that it's just these three Black women who are going to come through and change the world. We are one of thousands representing thousands of survivors, a lot of which don't want to say anything, and we're willing to take the brunt of the media pushback of this talking about being assaulted. But what's going to change society is when everyone feels that way. So when you're ready, when someone comes to you with their story, just point them in a direction that's safe and in a direction that will allow them agency. I would say the last point on top of, as we kind of said, like checking in with yourself, holding yourself accountable, doing the hard work within yourself, is the third part is to be a community member. I don't think any of this works, as you said, Coreen. I don't know how many times I can harp on that, that there's so many times that there are survivors who also are kind of fucked-up people. If I'm honest, I have, regardless of what that situation is, their survivor, and I'm there to assist them as much as I might want to speak up and say, "There's some other things that you said in what happened we will need to talk about later". You have to catch yourself victim blaming and say, what's the problem at hand? Yeah, there might be a lot of other stuff after we have this conversation, and after we get you the help for this specific instance that we need to look forward to. And that's being a community that's sticking around, you know. One of the worst parts about the cycle of violence is when the abuser has this person in this place to where they just have to drop you. And a lot of why I've kind of been so annoyed and trying not to be annoyed with the survivors in my own life. And in this idea of me, knowing that these survivors are not perfect and pushing myself to continue to be an advocate either way. What I don't believe to be revolutionary is to judge somebody for something you don't agree with. It's not revolutionary to tell somebody that where they come from is not valid, and it's not revolutionary to not stick up and stand up for people. So, you know, I kind of had to sit and ask myself, am I even revolutionary? Am I thinking? And in my practice, and in my way of moving forward? Or am I just perpetuating the same bullshit things.

So yeah, those are my three biggest things. If you know of any resources that are at your campus speak about them, have them on you. I used to love the people who would walk around and have flyers and stuff in their backpacks. I love those. I also love an Instagram page. I love to send people Instagram pages. That's also a really good resource. But yeah, stick up for yourself, and you'll learn how to stick up for others and believe them the first time.

Coreen H.: True. Sure! Sure.

Taylor W.: Well, that's it.

Exercise 5.1: Transcript debrief

Objectives: This discussion exercise can be used to expand participants' understandings of rape culture; campus culture; personal bias; racialized and queer personal narratives; group histories and storytelling.

Instructions:

1. Tell the learners and facilitators that the following exercise requires extended periods of talking and/or communicating stories. Please ask them to move to more comfortable positions and/or comfortable people.
2. Next, offer a myriad of participation methods within the activity. Some may choose to participate in silence, virtually, in person, in writing, or not at all. If they ask to leave class please allow them to. Discuss that literature is multimodal (comes in many different forms) and so will the work. Playlists, menus, photos, art, video, and other forms are encouraged!
3. Have participants decide whether or not they will discuss in small groups or the entire group.
4. Prompt listed and unlisted story prompts about any topic surrounding something inherently "group" to the

participants. Write, record, or document the beginning, middle, and end of the narrative.
5. If the participants wish to do so, make time before the end to share stories.

Discussion topic themes and questions

1. Campus community

a. How does university policy reinforce rape culture, heteronormativity, or patriarchy?
b. Do you think those on your campus would protect queer survivors or queer survivors of color?
c. Are there representatives on campus who could assist with calling out instances of rape culture?

2. Personal bias

a. When have you wrongly assumed something about someone? What were the consequences of the negative assumption?
b. What implicit biases can you identify in your own decision making (assumption of ability, stereotypes, etc.)?
c. Which of your own identities are you most interested in learning more about or discovering further?

3. Transcription-specific follow-up

a. Which moments of the conversation shocked you?

b. Have you encountered rape culture while on campus?
c. What were some moments or experiences you identify with?

References

Bedera, N. (2020). Trump's new rule governing college sex assault is nearly impossible for survivors to use. That's the point. *Time Magazine*. [Online] Available at: https://time.com/5836774/trump-new-title-ix-rules/.

Blackburn Center. (n.d.). *Teen issues*. [Online] Available at: www.blackburncenter.org/teen-issues [Accessed November 13, 2023].

The Combahee River Collective. (1977). *The Combahee River Collective Statement: Black Feminist Organizing in the Seventies and Eighties*. 1st ed. Albany, NY: Kitchen Table: Women of Color Press.

CNN. (2022). The Title IX Law Goes Beyond Gender Equality in Sports. Here's How. [YouTube] Available at: www.youtube.com/watch?v=sEgw_yRGV_k [Accessed November 13, 2023].

Hartman, S. V. (1997). *Scenes of Subjection: Terror, Slavery, and Self-making in Nineteenth-Century America*. New York: Oxford University Press.

Illinois University Library. (n.d.). Queer theory: Background. Available at: https://guides.library.illinois.edu/queertheory/background [Accessed August 17, 2023].

KnowyourIX.org. (n.d.). *Know your IX. Title IX protections for LGBTQ students*. Available at: https://knowyourix.org/college-resources/title-ix-protections-lgbtq-students/ [Accessed July 19, 2023].

Kosciw, J. G., Clark, C. M., & Menard, L. (2022). *The 2021 National School Climate Survey: The Experiences of LGBTQ+ Youth in Our Nation's Schools*. New York: GLSEN.

RAINN. (n.d.). *LGBTQ survivors of sexual violence*. [Online] Available at: www.rainn.org/articles/lgbtq-survivors-sexual-violence [Accessed March 6, 2024].

Rutgers, The State University of New Jersey. (n.d.). *History of women in the U.S. congress*. Available at: https://cawp.rutgers.edu/facts/levels-office/congress/history-women-us-congress (Accessed August 17, 2023).

Staurowsky, E. J., Flowers, C. L., Busuvis, E., Darvin, L., & Welch, N. (2022). 50 years of Title IX: We're not done yet. [Online] Women's Sports Foundation. Available at: www.womenssportsfoundation.org/wp-content/uploads/2022/05/13_Low-Res_Title-IX-50-Report.pdf [Accessed March 21, 2024].

Torraiva, K. (2018). "UTSA students' push aginst 'rape culture' has murky aftermath". *San Antonio Express-News*. [Online] Available at: www.expressnews.com/news/education/article/UTSA-students-push-against-rape-culture-13472492.php [Accessed March 21, 2024].

UN Women, Virtual Knowledge Centre to End Violence against Women and Girls. (2011). *Survivor-centred approach*. [Online] Available at: www.endvawnow.org/en/articles/652-survivor-centred-approach.html [Accessed November 13, 2023].

US Department of Education. (2023). *Fact sheet: U.S. Department of Education's proposed change to its Title IX regulations on students' eligibility for athletic teams*. [Online] Available at: www.ed.gov/news/press-releases/fact-sheet-us-department-educations-proposed-change-its-title-ix-regulations-students-eligibility-athletic-teams [Accessed July 19, 2023].

Winslow, B. (n.d.). The impact of Title IX. The Gilder Lehrman Institute of American History. [Online] Gilder Lehrman. Available at: www.gilderlehrman.org/history-resources/essays/impact-title-ix. [Accessed October 16, 2023].

Zeigler, C. & Webb, K. (2022). These 36 trans athletes have competed openly in college. [Online] Outsports. Available at: www.outsports.com/trans/2022/1/7/22850789/trans-athletes-college-ncaa-lia-thomas [Accessed November 13, 2023].

Recommended further reading

Bean, L. ed. (2018). *Written on the Body: Letters from Trans and Non-Binary Survivors of Sexual Assault and Domestic Violence.* London: Jessica Kingsley Publishers.

Index

ChangeRapeCulture 2, 9, 33, 35, 47–49, 53, 60, 68, 75

Combahee River Collective 22–23, 53

culture 21, 37, 58, 62, 72

education 2, 5, 7–8, 23, 54

gender 1–2, 4–8, 10, 34–35, 47

LGBTQIA2S+ 5, 7–8, 10–12, 18, 23–24, 49, 53, 62–65, 67, 74, 78, 80

rhetoric 49, 53–54

sexual violence viii, ix, x–1, 4, 8–9, 11–12, 16, 23–25, 32–34, 37, 49, 53–54, 57–59, 61, 67–68, 80–81

stereotype 11, 34, 80

www.ingramcontent.com/pod-product-compliance
Lightning Source LLC
Chambersburg PA
CBHW070809230426

43665CB00017B/2545